HISTORY'S MOST INFLUENTIAL INVENTORS

I0801700

FROM THE Late 1800s TO THE Early 1900s

Ferdinand von Zeppelin to Reginald Fessenden

EDITED BY ROBERT CURLEY

Britannica® Educational Publishing

IN ASSOCIATION WITH

ROSEN EDUCATIONAL SERVICES

Published in 2025 by Britannica Educational Publishing
(a trademark of Encyclopædia Britannica, Inc.)
in association with Rosen Educational Services, LLC
2544 Clinton Street, Buffalo, NY 14224.

Distributed exclusively by Rosen Educational Services.
For a listing of additional Britannica Educational Publishing titles, call toll free (800) 237-9932.

First Edition

Britannica Educational Publishing
Michael I. Levy: Executive Editor
Marilyn L. Barton: Senior Coordinator, Production Control
Steven Bosco: Director, Editorial Technologies
Lisa S. Braucher: Senior Producer and Data Editor
Yvette Charboneau: Senior Copy Editor
Kathy Nakamura: Manager, Media Acquisition
Robert Curley: Manager, Science and Technology

Editor: Greg Roza
Book design: Michael Flynn

Photo credits: Cover https://en.wikipedia.org/wiki/File:George_Washington_Carver_c1910_-_Restoration.jpg; p. 6 https://en.m.wikipedia.org/wiki/File:LZ_130_Graf_Zeppelin_in_flight.jpg; p. 8 https://en.m.wikipedia.org/wiki/File:Bildnis_Ferdinand_von_Zeppelin.png; p. 11 https://commons.wikimedia.org/wiki/File:Maxim,_Cassier_and_Smith_with_Machine_Gun_for_Germany_-_Cassier%27s_1895-04_(cropped).png; p. 17 https://commons.wikimedia.org/wiki/File:Gottlieb_Daimler_1890s2.jpg; p. 29 https://commons.wikimedia.org/wiki/File:Thomas_Edison2.jpg; p. 34 https://commons.wikimedia.org/wiki/File:Alexander_Graham_Bell_by_E._J._Holmes,_1892,_albumen_silver_print,_from_the_National_Portrait_Gallery_-_NPG-NPG_2010_28GrahamBell-000001.jpg; pp. 40, 50 Everett Collection/Shutterstock.com; p. 45 https://commons.wikimedia.org/wiki/File:Tesla_raio_x_02.jpg; p. 55 https://commons.wikimedia.org/wiki/File:Dr._James_Naismith.jpg.

Cataloging-in-Publication Data

Names: Curley, Robert, 1955-.
Title: From the late 1800s to the early 1900s: Ferdinand von Zeppelin to Reginald Fessenden / edited by Robert Curley.
Description: New York : Britannica Educational Publishing, in Association with Rosen Educational Services, 2025. | Series: History's most influential inventors | Includes glossary and index.
Identifiers: ISBN 9781641900935 (library bound) | ISBN 9781641900928 (pbk) | ISBN 9781641900942 (ebook)
Subjects: LCSH: Inventors--Biography. | Inventions--History.
Classification: LCC T39.F766 2025 | DDC 609.2'2--dc23

Manufactured in the United States of America

CPSIA Compliance Information: Batch #CSBRIT25. For further information contact Rosen Publishing at 1-800-237-9932.

CONTENTS

Introduction. 4
Ferdinand von Zeppelin 6
Hiram Maxim. 10
John P. Holland 12
Karl Benz and Gottlieb Daimler . . .14
Wilhelm Conrad Röntgen 18
Thomas Edison 19
Alexander Graham Bell 33
Otto Lilienthal. 39
Emil Berliner 41
Nikola Tesla 43
Rudolf Diesel 48
George Washington Carver. 49
James A. Naismith. 54
Auguste and Louis Lumière 56
Reginald Fessenden. 57
Glossary. 60
For More Information 61
Index 62

Introduction

"Nothing is impossible. We merely don't know how to do it yet."
—Thomas Edison (1847–1931)

Life has been transformed over the years through the efforts of the men and women who had the brilliance, diligence, and creativity to come up with new and better ways of doing things. This book focuses on the inventions of people who lived in the late 1800s and the early 1900s. As detailed throughout these pages, their inventions spawned many more inventions, speeding up the pace of progress even further.

The 19th century was a time of incredible innovation and change. There was no lack of invention before then; it was just the pace of invention that sped up significantly after that time. Some of the individual inventors profiled here were extremely prolific. For example, Thomas Edison was issued some 1,093 U.S. patents during his career.

Intelligence and curiosity are unquestionably important assets for inventors, but having an advanced degree—or even a formal education—has never been a prerequisite. Edison studied at home with his mother. George Washington Carver, who began life as an enslaved person, taught himself to read from the only book he possessed—*Webster's Elementary Spelling Book*.

Sometimes the process of invention was painstakingly slow and required many hours of trial and error. In Edison's quest to develop electric lighting, he experimented with 6,000 different materials before finally discovering a filament (carbonized thread) that would stay lit for many hours inside a bulb without burning up. It's no wonder that the famous quote "Genius is 99 percent perspiration and 1 percent inspiration" is attributed to him.

Inventors clearly improved life by keeping people healthier, helping them to communicate and work more efficiently, and allowing them to travel farther. This book recognizes not only the inventors whose work changed the course of human life, but also those whose ideas paved the way for future generations of inventors. Alexander Graham Bell's fascination with the idea of sending sound down a wire from the speaker to the listener gave birth to the telephone, which ultimately led to the cell phone, fax machine, modem, and a communication system that now links the entire globe.

Inventors themselves have sometimes been skeptical about the ability of their own creations to endure. Despite the public excitement that greeted their Cinèmatographe motion picture machine when it was released in 1895, the Lumière brothers felt that their invention was just a fad. In fact, Louis Lumière referred to the cinema as "an invention without a future." In spite of the Lumière brothers' initial cynicism, film endures as one of the most popular art forms today.

So many inventors have made important contributions in this time period that to mention them all here would far exceed the space limitations of this book. The figures who have been included are among the greatest and most prolific inventors of all time. They were selected because their inventions have altered the course of people's lives and have left an indelible stamp on human history.

FERDINAND VON ZEPPELIN

(b. July 8, 1838, Konstanz, Baden [now in Ger.]—d. March 8, 1917, Charlottenburg, near Berlin)

Ferdinand Adolf August Heinrich, Graf (count) von Zeppelin, was the first notable builder of rigid dirigible airships, for which his surname is still a popular generic term.

Zeppelin received a military commission in 1858. He made the first of several balloon ascensions at Saint Paul, Minnesota, while acting as a military observer (1863) for the Union Army during the American Civil War. He saw military action in 1866 during the Seven Weeks' War and

Rigid dirigible airships were used for bombing runs during World War I. After that, airplane technology outpaced zeppelin technology for militaries.

in 1870–71 during the Franco-German War, serving successively in the armies of Württemberg, Prussia, and imperial Germany. He retired in 1890 and devoted the rest of his life to the creation of the rigid airship for which he is known.

Zeppelin struggled for 10 years to produce his lighter-than-air craft. In previous experimentation on dirigibles, hydrogen and illuminating gas were substituted for hot air to provide buoyancy, and a motor was mounted on a gas bag fitted with propellers and rudders. Small steam engines were tried, but as progress took place first electric motors and, in Germany after 1888, gasoline engines were used. The problem remained how to maintain the shape of the gas bags. Fully filled with gas under the right pressure, a cigar shape could be maintained and steered; but a partially deflated bag was almost impossible to direct. It was Zeppelin who first saw clearly that maintaining a steerable shape was essential, so he created a rigid but very light trussed and covered frame supported by internal gas cells. This solved many of the steering problems, but how to give the frame sufficient strength to deal with torque introduced by air currents in storms continued to be a severe challenge.

The initial flight (July 2, 1900) of the LZ-1 (for Luftschiff Zeppelin) from a floating hangar on Lake Constance, near Friedrichshafen, Germany, was not entirely successful. The LZ-l flew for 17 minutes before sinking to thc surfacc of thc lakc and impaling itsclf on a buoy that punctured the gas bag. Nevertheless, it had the effect of promoting the airship to the degree that public subscriptions and donations thereafter funded the count's work. After years of cautious changes in design Zeppelin was ready in 1908 with the LZ-4, 446 feet (134 m) long and carrying more than half a million cubic feet (14,000 cubic meters) of hydrogen. On July 1 he achieved 12 hours of

Ferdiand von Zeppelin sat for this photograph in 1917, shortly before his death that same year.

sustained flight at a speed of 40 miles (65 km) per hour over central Switzerland.

With the LZ-5, the dirigible became a potentially practical air transport. A passenger service known as Delag (Deutsche-Luftschiffahrts AG) was established in 1910, becoming the first well-financed air transportation company. In the five-year period up to the outbreak of World War I Delag made 1,588 flights, safely carrying 34,228 passengers, covering a total of some 170,000 miles (270,000 km). During the war 88 zeppelins (as they came to be known) were constructed for military purposes, among which was the introduction of the first sustained distant aerial warfare, which included the bombing of London and a flight from Yambol, Bulgaria, of 2,800 miles (4,500 km) toward German East Africa.

Zeppelin died before attaining his goal of transcontinental flight. However, when Germany was permitted to return to civilian flying in the mid-1920s, the Luftschiffsbau-Zeppelin (Zeppelin Company) began planning a transatlantic passenger voyage. In 1928 the company completed a new airship, the *Graf Zeppelin*, which inaugurated transatlantic flight service. By the time of its decommissioning in 1937 the *Graf Zeppelin* had made 590 flights, including 144 ocean crossings, and had flown more than 1 million miles (1.6 million km). In 1929 the craft covered about 21,500 miles (34,600 km) in a round-the-world flight that was completed in 21 days, 5 hours, and 54 minutes (of which only 47 hours had been spent on the ground), yielding an average speed of some 70 miles (112 km) per hour. On July 2, 1996, the 96th anniversary of the inaugural flight of the LZ-1, the Zeppelin Museum Friedrichshafen was opened in a restored railway station on the shore of Lake Constance.

HIRAM MAXIM

(b. Feb. 5, 1840, Sangerville, Maine, U.S.—d. Nov. 24, 1916, London, Eng.)

Hiram Stevens Maxim was a prolific inventor best known for the Maxim machine gun.

The eldest son of a farmer who was a locally notable mechanic, Maxim was apprenticed at 14 to a carriage maker. Exhibiting an early genius for invention, he obtained his first patent in 1866, for a hair-curling iron. His iron was followed by a device for generating illuminating gas and a locomotive headlight; in 1878 he was hired as chief engineer of the United States Electric Lighting Company, the first such company in the United States. In that post he produced a basic invention, a method of manufacturing carbon filaments. In 1881 he exhibited an electric pressure regulator at the Paris Exposition.

Maxim's interest in the problem of automatic weapons led him to settle in London. In 1884 he produced the first satisfactory fully automatic machine gun, employing the recoil energy of the bullet to unlock the breechblock from the barrel, extract and eject the fired case from the gun, and store sufficient energy in a main spring to push the bolt forward, pick up a fresh round, load the chamber, and lock the piece. Both barrel and breechblock, locked together, recoiled a short distance to the rear; then the barrel was stopped and the block continued back alone. If the trigger was held in firing position, the weapon would continue to fire until it expended all of its ammunition. Rounds were fed to the gun on belts, which could be clipped together to provide continuous fire, and overheating was solved by surrounding the barrel in a metal jacket in which water was circulated from a separate container. To improve the efficiency of his gun, Maxim developed his

Maxin (left) shows two German scientists his machine gun.

own smokeless powder, cordite.

Maxim's salesmen provided armies with guns in any caliber, usually matching their current rifle cartridge, and within a few years every army was equipped with Maxim guns or adaptations. The light weight of the guns, made possible because the cartridge was the sole source of power, allowed them to be operated by special infantry units. In warfare, machine guns of the Maxim type had a destructive power never seen before. In the 1890s, British infantry units used Maxim guns, fabricated under contract by Vickers Sons, to cut down hordes of poorly armed rebels in Africa and Afghanistan. In World War I, a few of them could cause thousands of casualties. Their defensive fire so limited the offensive power of infantry that the entire Western Front, from the Swiss border to the English Channel, became one vast siege operation.

In the 1890s Maxim experimented with airplanes, producing one powered by a light steam engine that successfully rose from the ground; he recognized that the real solution to flight was the internal-combustion engine but did not attempt to develop it. His hundreds of patents in the United States and Great Britain included a mousetrap, an automatic sprinkling system, an automatic steam-powered water pump, vacuum pumps, engine governors, and gas motors.

His Maxim Gun Company, founded in 1884, was later absorbed into Vickers, Ltd., of which he became a director. In 1900 he became a naturalized British subject, and in 1901 he was knighted by Queen Victoria.

JOHN P. HOLLAND

(b. Feb. 29, 1840, Liscannor, County Clare, Ire.—d. Aug. 12, 1914, Newark, N.J., U.S.)

John Philip Holland designed and built the first underwater vessel accepted by the U.S. Navy. He is considered to be the father of the modern submarine.

Educated at Limerick, Holland taught school until 1872 in Ireland and in 1873 emigrated to the United States. Settling in Paterson, New Jersey, he taught there until 1879, when, with financial support from the Irish Fenian Society (who hoped to use submarines against Britain), he built the *Fenian Ram*, a small sub that proved a limited success in a test run. Holland's early submarines were significant in combining water ballast with horizontal rudders for diving. In 1895 his J.P. Holland Torpedo Boat Company received a contract from the U.S. Navy to build a submarine. This was to be the *Plunger*, propelled by steam on the surface and by electricity when submerged. The craft underwent many design changes and finally was abandoned before completion. Holland returned the funds advanced by the navy and built his next submarine (his sixth) at his own expense. This was the *Holland*, a 53-foot (16 m) craft launched in 1897 and accepted by the navy in 1900. For underwater propulsion the *Holland* had an electric motor, and it was propelled on the surface by a gasoline engine. The *Holland* had a surface speed of 7 knots (nautical miles per hour; 13 km per hour). The submarine's armament consisted of a bow torpedo tube, for which three torpedoes were carried, and two dynamite guns. With its nine-man crew the *Holland* was a successful boat; it was modified many times to test different arrangements of propellers, diving planes, rudders, and other equipment. The U.S. government ordered six more.

Holland's final years were marked by litigation with his financial backers. One of his last inventions was an apparatus designed to enable sailors to escape from damaged submarines.

KARL BENZ AND GOTTLIEB DAIMLER

Most authorities are inclined to honor Karl Benz and Gottlieb Daimler of Germany as the most important pioneer contributors to the gasoline-engine automobile. Benz ran his first car in 1885; Daimler in 1886. Although there is no reason to believe that Benz had ever seen a motor vehicle before he made his own, he and Daimler had been preceded by Étienne Lenoir in France and Siegfried Marcus in Austria, in 1862 and 1864–65, respectively, but neither Lenoir nor Marcus had persisted. Benz and Daimler did persist—to such purpose that their successor firm of Daimler AG can trace its origins back to the 1890s and claim, with the Peugeot SA firm of France, to be one of the oldest automobile-manufacturing firms in the world. Oddly, Benz and Daimler never met.

Karl Benz

(b. Nov. 25, 1844, Karlsruhe, Baden [now in Ger.]—d. April 4, 1929, Ladenburg, near Mannheim, Ger.)

Karl Friedrich Benz was a mechanical engineer who designed and built the world's first practical automobile to be powered by an internal-combustion engine. In 1883 he founded Benz & Co. in Mannheim to build stationary internal-combustion engines, but he was completely dedicated to the proposition that the internal-combustion engine would supersede the horse and revolutionize the world's transportation. He persisted in his efforts to build a gasoline-fueled vehicle in the face of many obstacles, including lack of money to the point of poverty and the bitter objections of his associates, who considered him unbalanced on the subject.

Benz ran his first car, a three-wheeler powered by a two-cycle, one-cylinder engine, on a happy and triumphant day early in 1885. He circled a cinder track beside his small factory, his workmen running beside the car, his wife running too, clapping her hands; the little machine made four circuits of the track, stalling only twice before a broken chain stopped it. Even Max Rose, Benz's skeptical partner, whose money had made the car possible, conceded that he was mildly impressed; but he remained convinced to the end of his association with Benz that there was no future in the horseless carriage. The original Benz three-wheeled vehicle, the *Motorwagen*, is now preserved in Munich. Although it first ran early in 1885, its design was not patented until January 29, 1886.

In his way, Benz was dogmatic and reactionary; he objected to redesign of his original cars, and some authorities believe that he was never really convinced that his original concepts had been improved upon. Gradually, however, the soundness of his design and the quality and care that went into the material and the construction of his cars bore weight, and they sold well. He made his first sale to a Parisian named Émile Roger in 1888. That year he was employing some 50 workmen to build the tricycle car. The company completed its first four-wheeled automobile in 1893 and produced the first of a series of racing cars in 1899. In 1926 the Benz company merged with Daimler-Motoren-Gesellschaft to form Daimler-Benz, maker of Mercedes-Benz automobiles. Benz had left the firm about 1906 to organize C. Benz Söhne, Ladenburg, with his sons, Eugen and Richard.

Gottlieb Daimler

(b. March 17, 1834, Schorndorf, Württemberg [now in Ger.]—d. March 6, 1900, Cannstatt, near Stuttgart)

Mechanical engineer Gottlieb Wilhelm Daimler became a major figure in the early history of the automotive industry. Gunsmithing was his first vocation, and he showed marked talent, but he abandoned the trade to go to engineering school, studying in Germany, England, and France. In Germany he worked for various engineering and machining concerns, including the Karlsruhe Maschinenbaugesellschaft, a firm that much earlier had employed Benz.

In 1872 Daimler became technical director in the firm of Nikolaus A. Otto, the man who had invented the four-stroke internal-combustion engine. Otto's firm was then building stationary gasoline engines. During the next decade, important work was done on the four-stroke engine. Daimler brought in several brilliant researchers, among them Wilhelm Maybach, but in 1882 both Daimler and Maybach resigned because of Daimler's conviction that Otto did not understand the potential of the internal-combustion engine. They set up a shop in Bad Cannstatt and built an air-cooled, one-cylinder engine in 1885. The first high-speed internal-combustion engine, it was designed to run at 900 revolutions per minute (rpm). For comparison, Benz's first tricycle engine had operated at only 250 rpm. Daimler and Maybach used one of their early gasoline engines on a wooden bicycle fitted with an outrigger, which first ran on November 10, 1885. This may have been the first motorcycle in the world. The next year the first Daimler four-wheeled road vehicle was made: a horse-drawn carriage modified to be driven by a one-cylinder engine.

Daimler appears to have believed that the first phase of the automobile era would be a mass conversion of carriages to engine drive; Benz apparently thought of the motorcar as a separate device. Nevertheless, Daimler and Maybach's 1889 car was a departure from previous

This photograph of Gottlieb Daimler was taken in the 1890s.

practice. Designed from the start as an automobile and not a carriage, it was based on a framework of light tubing; it had the engine in the rear; its wheels were driven by a belt; and it was steered by a tiller. Remarkably, it had four speeds. This car had obvious commercial value, and in the following year the Daimler Motoren-Gesellschaft was founded. The British Daimler automobile was started as a manufactory licensed by the German company but later became quite independent of it. (To distinguish machines made by the two firms in the early years, the German cars are usually referred to as Cannstatt-Daimlers.) In 1899 the firm built the first Mercedes car. The Daimler and Benz firms were merged in 1926, and products thereafter have been sold under the name Mercedes-Benz. This practice continued even during the 1998–2007 merger with the American firm Chrysler Corporation to form DaimlerChrysler AG.

WILHELM CONRAD RÖNTGEN

(b. March 27, 1845, Lennep, Prussia [now Remscheid, Ger.]—d. Feb. 10, 1923, Munich, Ger.)

Wilhelm Conrad Röntgen was a German physicist who was a recipient of the first Nobel Prize for Physics, in 1901, for his discovery of X-rays, which heralded the age of modern physics and revolutionized diagnostic medicine.

Röntgen studied at the Polytechnic in Zürich and then was professor of physics at the universities of Strasbourg (1876–79), Giessen (1879–88), Würzburg (1888–1900), and Munich (1900–20). His research also included work on elasticity, capillary action of fluids, specific heats of gases, conduction of heat in crystals, absorption of heat by gases, and piezoelectricity.

In 1895, while experimenting with electric current flow in a partially evacuated glass tube (cathode-ray tube), Röntgen observed that a nearby piece of barium platinocyanide gave off light when the tube was in operation. He theorized that when the cathode rays (electrons) struck the glass wall of the tube, some unknown radiation was formed that traveled across the room, struck the chemical, and caused the fluorescence. Further investigation revealed that paper, wood, and aluminum, among other materials, are transparent to this new form of radiation. He found that it affected photographic plates, and, since it did not noticeably exhibit any properties of light, such as reflection or refraction, he mistakenly thought the rays were unrelated to light. In view of its uncertain nature, he called the phenomenon X-radiation, though it also became known as Röntgen radiation. He took the first X-ray photographs, of the interiors of metal objects and of the bones in his wife's hand.

Röntgen's discovery of X-rays was met with worldwide scientific and popular excitement. Within months of the discovery there was extensive literature on the subject: a British surgeon had localized a bullet in a boy's wrist before operating; stones in the urinary bladder and gallbladder had been demonstrated; and fractures had been displayed. Along with the discoveries of radioactivity (1896) and the electron (1897), the discovery of X-rays ushered in the study of the atomic world and the era of modern physics.

THOMAS EDISON

(b. Feb. 11, 1847, Milan, Ohio, U.S.—d. Oct. 18, 1931, West Orange, N.J.)

Thomas Alva Edison was an American inventor who, singly or jointly, held a world record 1,093 U.S.

patents. In addition, he created the world's first industrial research laboratory.

Edison was the quintessential American inventor in the era of Yankee ingenuity. He began his career in 1863, in the adolescence of the telegraph industry, when virtually the only source of electricity was primitive batteries putting out a low-voltage current. Before he died, in 1931, he had played a critical role in introducing the modern age of electricity. From his laboratories and workshops emanated the phonograph, the carbon-button transmitter for the telephone speaker and microphone, the incandescent lamp, a revolutionary generator of unprecedented efficiency, the first commercial electric light and power system, an experimental electric railroad, and key elements of motion-picture apparatus, as well as a host of other inventions.

Early Years

Edison was the seventh and last child—the fourth surviving—of Samuel Edison Jr. and Nancy Elliot Edison. At an early age he developed hearing problems, which have been variously attributed but were most likely due to a familial tendency to mastoiditis. Whatever the cause, Edison's deafness strongly influenced his behavior and career, providing the motivation for many of his inventions.

In 1854 Samuel Edison became the lighthouse keeper and carpenter on the Fort Gratiot military post near Port Huron, Michigan, where the family lived in a substantial home. Alva, as the inventor was known until his second marriage, entered school there and attended sporadically for five years. He was imaginative and inquisitive, but because much instruction was by rote and he had difficulty hearing, he was bored and was labeled a misfit. To compensate, he became an avid and omnivorous reader.

Edison's lack of formal schooling was not unusual. At the time of the Civil War the average American had attended school a total of 434 days—little more than two years' schooling by today's standards.

In 1859 Edison quit school and began working as a trainboy on the railroad between Detroit and Port Huron. Four years earlier, the Michigan Central had initiated the commercial application of the telegraph by using it to control the movement of its trains, and the Civil War brought a vast expansion of transportation and communication. Edison took advantage of the opportunity to learn telegraphy and in 1863 became an apprentice telegrapher.

Messages received on the initial Morse telegraph were inscribed as a series of dots and dashes on a strip of paper that was decoded and read, so Edison's partial deafness was no handicap. Receivers were increasingly being equipped with a sounding key, however, enabling telegraphers to "read" messages by the clicks. The transformation of telegraphy to an auditory art left Edison more and more disadvantaged during his six-year career as an itinerant telegrapher in the Midwest, the South, Canada, and New England. Amply supplied with ingenuity and insight, he devoted much of his energy toward improving the inchoate equipment and inventing devices to facilitate some of the tasks that his physical limitations made difficult. By January 1869 he had made enough progress with a duplex telegraph (a device capable of transmitting two messages simultaneously on one wire) and a printer, which converted electrical signals to letters, that he abandoned telegraphy for full-time invention and entrepreneurship.

Edison moved to New York City, where he initially went into partnership with Frank L. Pope, a noted electrical expert, to produce the Edison Universal Stock Printer and other printing telegraphs. Between 1870 and 1875 he worked out of Newark, New Jersey, and was involved in a variety of partnerships and complex transactions in the fiercely competitive and convoluted telegraph industry, which was dominated by the Western Union Telegraph Company. As an independent entrepreneur he was available to the highest bidder and played both sides against the middle. During this period he worked on improving an automatic telegraph system for Western Union's rivals. The automatic telegraph, which recorded messages by means of a chemical reaction engendered by the electrical transmissions, proved of limited commercial success, but the work advanced Edison's knowledge of chemistry and laid the basis for his development of the electric pen and mimeograph, both important devices in the early office machine industry, and indirectly led to the discovery of the phonograph. Under the aegis of Western Union he devised the quadruplex, capable of transmitting four messages simultaneously over one wire, but railroad baron and Wall Street financier Jay Gould, Western Union's bitter rival, snatched the quadruplex from the telegraph company's grasp in December 1874 by paying Edison more than $100,000 in cash, bonds, and stock, one of the larger payments for any invention up to that time. Years of litigation followed.

Menlo Park

Although Edison was a sharp bargainer, he was a poor financial manager, often spending and giving away money more rapidly than he earned it. In 1871 he married 16-year-old Mary Stilwell, who was as improvident in household matters as he was in business, and before the end of 1875 they were in financial difficulties. To reduce his costs and the temptation to spend money, Edison brought his now-widowed father from Port Huron to build a 2 1/2-story laboratory and machine shop in the rural environs of

Menlo Park, New Jersey—12 miles south of Newark—where he moved in March 1876. Accompanying him were two key associates, Charles Batchelor and John Kruesi. Batchelor, born in Manchester in 1845, was a master mechanic and draftsman who complemented Edison perfectly and served as his "ears" on such projects as the phonograph and telephone. He was also responsible for fashioning the drawings that Kruesi, a Swiss-born machinist, translated into models.

Edison experienced his finest hours at Menlo Park. While experimenting on an underwater cable for the automatic telegraph, he found that the electrical resistance and conductivity of carbon (then called plumbago) varied according to the pressure it was under. This was a major theoretical discovery, which enabled Edison to devise a "pressure relay" using carbon rather than the usual magnets to vary and balance electric currents. In February 1877 Edison began experiments designed to produce a pressure relay that would amplify and improve the audibility of the telephone, a device that Edison and others had studied but which Alexander Graham Bell was the first to patent, in 1876. By the end of 1877 Edison had developed the carbon-button transmitter that is still used in telephone speakers and microphones.

The Phonograph

Edison invented many items, including the carbon transmitter, in response to specific demands for new products or improvements. But he also had the gift of serendipity: when some unexpected phenomenon was observed, he did not hesitate to halt work in progress and turn off course in a new direction. This was how, in 1877, he achieved his most original discovery, the phonograph. Because the telephone was considered a variation of acoustic telegraphy, Edison during the summer of 1877 was attempting to devise for it, as he had for the automatic telegraph, a machine that would transcribe signals as they were received, in this instance in the form of the human voice, so that they could then be delivered as telegraph messages. (The telephone was not yet conceived as a general, person-to-person means of communication.) Some earlier researchers, notably the French inventor Léon Scott, had theorized that each sound, if it could be graphically recorded, would produce a distinct shape resembling shorthand, or phonography ("sound writing"), as it was then known. Edison hoped to reify this concept by employing a stylus-tipped carbon transmitter to make impressions on a strip of paraffined paper. To his astonishment, the scarcely visible indentations generated a vague reproduction of sound when the paper was pulled back beneath the stylus.

Edison unveiled the tinfoil phonograph, which replaced the strip of paper with a cylinder wrapped in tinfoil, in December 1877. It was greeted with incredulity. Indeed, a leading French scientist declared it to be the trick device of a clever ventriloquist. The public's amazement was quickly followed by universal acclaim. Edison was projected into worldwide prominence and was dubbed the Wizard of Menlo Park, although a decade passed before the phonograph was transformed from a laboratory curiosity into a commercial product.

The Electric Light

Another offshoot of the carbon experiments reached fruition sooner. Samuel Langley, Henry Draper, and other American scientists needed a highly sensitive instrument that could be used to measure minute temperature changes in heat emitted from the sun's corona during a solar eclipse along the Rocky Mountains on July 29, 1878. To satisfy those needs Edison devised a "microtasimeter" employing a carbon button. This was a time when great advances were being made in electric arc lighting, and during the expedition, which Edison accompanied, the men discussed the practicality of "subdividing" the intense arc lights so that electricity could be used for lighting in the same fashion as with small, individual gas "burners." The basic problem seemed to be to keep the burner, or bulb, from being consumed by preventing it from overheating. Edison thought he would be able to solve this by fashioning a microtasimeter-like device to control the current. He boldly announced that he would invent a safe, mild, and inexpensive electric light that would replace the gaslight.

The incandescent electric light had been the despair of inventors for 50 years, but Edison's past achievements commanded respect for his boastful prophecy. Thus, a syndicate of leading financiers, including J.P. Morgan and the Vanderbilts, established the Edison Electric Light Company and advanced him $30,000 for research and development. Edison proposed to connect his lights in a parallel circuit by subdividing the current, so that, unlike arc lights, which were connected in a series circuit, the failure of one light bulb would not cause a whole circuit to fail. Some eminent scientists predicted that such a circuit could never be feasible, but their findings were based on systems of lamps with low resistance—the only successful type of electric light at the time. Edison, however, determined that a bulb with high resistance would serve his purpose, and he began searching for a suitable one.

He had the assistance of 26-year-old Francis Upton, a graduate of Princeton University with an M.A. in science. Upton, who joined the laboratory force in December 1878, provided the mathematical and theoretical expertise that Edison himself lacked. (Edison later revealed, "At the time I experimented on the incandescent lamp I did not understand Ohm's law." On another occasion he said, "I do not depend on figures at all. I try an experiment and reason out the result, somehow, by methods which I could not explain.")

By the summer of 1879 Edison and Upton had made enough progress on a generator—which, by reverse action, could be employed as a motor—that Edison, beset by failed incandescent lamp experiments, considered offering a system of electric distribution for power, not light. By October Edison and his staff had achieved encouraging results with a complex, regulator-controlled vacuum bulb with a platinum filament, but the cost of the platinum would have made the incandescent light impractical. While experimenting with an insulator for the platinum wire, they discovered that, in the greatly improved vacuum they were now obtaining through advances made in the vacuum pump, carbon could be maintained for some time without elaborate regulatory apparatus. Advancing on the work of Joseph Wilson Swan, an English physicist, Edison found that a carbon filament provided a good light with the concomitant high resistance required for subdivision. Steady progress ensued from the first breakthrough in mid-October until the initial demonstration for the backers of the Edison Electric Light Company on December 3.

It was, nevertheless, not until the summer of 1880 that Edison determined that carbonized bamboo fiber made a satisfactory material for the filament, although the world's first operative lighting system had been installed on the steamship *Columbia* in April. The first commercial land-based "isolated" (single-building) incandescent system was placed in the New York printing firm of Hinds and Ketcham in January 1881. In the fall a temporary, demonstration central power system was installed at the Holborn

Viaduct in London, in conjunction with an exhibition at the Crystal Palace. Edison himself supervised the laying of the mains and installation of the world's first permanent, commercial central power system in lower Manhattan, which became operative in September 1882. Although the early systems were plagued by problems and many years passed before incandescent lighting powered by electricity from central stations made significant inroads into gas lighting, isolated lighting plants for such enterprises as hotels, theaters, and stores flourished—as did Edison's reputation as the world's greatest inventor.

One of the accidental discoveries made in the Menlo Park laboratory during the development of the incandescent light anticipated the British physicist J.J. Thomson's discovery of the electron 15 years later. In 1881–82 William J. Hammer, a young engineer in charge of testing the light globes, noted a blue glow around the positive pole in a vacuum bulb and a blackening of the wire and the bulb at the negative pole. This phenomenon was first called "Hammer's phantom shadow," but when Edison patented the bulb in 1883 it became known as the "Edison effect." Scientists later determined that this effect was explained by the thermionic emission of electrons from the hot to the cold electrode, and it became the basis of the electron tube and laid the foundation for the electronics industry.

Edison had moved his operations from Menlo Park to New York City when work commenced on the Manhattan power system. Increasingly, the Menlo Park property was used only as a summer home. In August 1884 Edison's wife, Mary, suffering from deteriorating health and subject to periods of mental derangement, died there of "congestion of the brain," apparently a tumor or hemorrhage. Her death and the move from Menlo Park roughly mark the halfway point of Edison's life.

The Edison Laboratory

A widower with three young children, Edison, on February 24, 1886, married 20-year-old Mina Miller, the daughter of a prosperous Ohio manufacturer. He purchased a hilltop estate in West Orange, New Jersey, for his new bride and constructed nearby a grand, new laboratory, which he intended to be the world's first true research facility. There, he produced the commercial phonograph, founded the motion-picture industry, and developed the alkaline storage battery. Nevertheless, Edison was past the peak of his productive period. A poor manager and organizer, he worked best in intimate, relatively unstructured surroundings with a handful of close associates and assistants; the West Orange laboratory was too sprawling and diversified for his talents. Furthermore, as a significant portion of the inventor's time was taken up by his new role of industrialist, which came with the commercialization of incandescent lighting and the phonograph, electrical developments were passing into the domain of university-trained mathematicians and scientists. Above all, for more than a decade Edison's energy was focused on a magnetic ore-mining venture that proved the unquestioned disaster of his career.

The first major endeavor at the new laboratory was the commercialization of the phonograph, a venture launched in 1887 after Alexander Graham Bell, his cousin Chichester, and Charles Tainter had developed the graphophone—an improved version of Edison's original device—which used waxed cardboard instead of tinfoil. Two years later, Edison announced that he had "perfected" the phonograph, although this was far from true. In fact, it was not until the late 1890s, after Edison had established production and recording facilities adjacent to the laboratory, that all the

Edison, shown here in 1922, won many awards during his life and after he died. In 1923, Edison won the very first "Edison Medal" from the American Institute of Electrical Engineers.

mechanical problems were overcome and the phonograph became a profitable proposition.

In the meantime, Edison conceived the idea of popularizing the phonograph by linking to it in synchronization a zoetrope, a device that gave the illusion of motion to photographs shot in sequence. He assigned the project to William K.L. Dickson, an employee interested in photography, in 1888. After studying the work of various European photographers who also were trying to record motion, Edison and Dickson succeeded in constructing a working camera and a viewing instrument, which were called, respectively, the Kinetograph and the Kinetoscope. Synchronizing sound and motion proved of such insuperable difficulty, however, that the concept of linking the two was abandoned, and the silent movie was born. Edison constructed at the laboratory the world's first motion-picture stage, nicknamed the "Black Maria," in 1893, and the following year Kinetoscopes, which had peepholes that allowed one person at a time to view the moving pictures, were introduced with great success. Rival inventors soon developed screen-projection systems that hurt the Kinetoscope's business, however, so Edison acquired a projector developed by Thomas Armat and introduced it as "Edison's latest marvel, the Vitascope."

Another derivative of the phonograph was the alkaline storage battery, which Edison began developing as a power source for the phonograph at a time when most homes still lacked electricity. Although it was 20 years before all the difficulties with the battery were solved, by 1909 Edison was a principal supplier of batteries for submarines and electric vehicles and had even formed a company for the manufacture of electric automobiles. In 1912 Henry Ford, one of Edison's greatest admirers, asked him to design a battery for the self-starter, to be introduced on the Model T. Ford's request led to a continuing relationship between these two Americans, and in October 1929 he staged a 50th-anniversary celebration of the incandescent light that turned into a universal apotheosis for Edison himself.

Most of Edison's successes involved electricity or communication, but throughout the late 1880s and early 1890s the Edison Laboratory's top priority was the magnetic ore-separator. Edison had first worked on the separator when he was searching for platinum for use in the experimental incandescent lamp. The device was supposed to cull platinum from iron-bearing sand. During the 1880s iron ore prices rose to unprecedented heights, so that it appeared that, if the separator could extract the iron from unusable low-grade ores, then abandoned mines might profitably be placed back in production. Edison purchased or acquired rights to 145 old mines in the east and established a large pilot plant at the Ogden mine, near Ogdensburg, New Jersey. He was never able to surmount the engineering problems or work the bugs out of the system, however, and when ore prices plummeted in the mid-1890s he gave up on the idea. By then he had liquidated all but a small part of his holdings in the General Electric Company, sometimes at very low prices, and had become more and more separated from the electric lighting field.

Failure could not discourage Edison's passion for invention, however. Although none of his later projects were as successful as his earlier ones, he continued to work even in his 80s.

Assessment

The thrust of Edison's work may be seen in the clustering of his patents: 389 for electric light and power, 195 for the phonograph, 150 for the telegraph, 141 for storage batteries, and 34 for the telephone. His life and achievements epitomize the ideal of applied research. He always invented for necessity, with the object of devising something new that he could manufacture. The basic principles he discovered were derived from practical experiments, invariably by chance, thus reversing the orthodox concept of pure research leading to applied research.

Edison's role as a machine shop operator and small manufacturer was crucial to his success as an inventor. Unlike other scientists and inventors of the time, who had limited means and lacked a support organization, Edison ran an inventive establishment. He was the antithesis of the lone inventive genius, although his deafness enforced on him an isolation conducive to conception. His lack of managerial ability was, in an odd way, also a stimulant. As his own boss, he plunged ahead on projects more prudent men would have shunned, then tended to dissipate the fruits of his inventiveness, so that he was both free and forced to develop new ideas. Few men have matched him in the positiveness of his thinking. Edison never questioned whether something might be done, only how.

Edison's career, the fulfillment of the American dream of rags-to-riches through hard work and intelligence, made him a folk hero to his countrymen. In temperament he was an uninhibited egotist, at once a tyrant to his employees and their most entertaining companion, so that there was never a dull moment with him. He was charismatic and courted publicity, but he had difficulty socializing and neglected his family. His shafts at the expense of the "long-haired" fraternity of theorists sometimes led formally trained scientists to deprecate him as anti-intellectual; yet he employed as his aides, at various times, a number of eminent mathematical physicists, such as Nikola Tesla and A.E. Kennelly. The contradictory nature of his forceful personality, as well as such eccentricities as his ability to catnap anywhere, contributed to his legendary status. By the time he was in his middle 30s Edison was said to be the best-known American in the world. When he died he was venerated and mourned as the man who, more than any other, had laid the basis for the technological and social revolution of the modern electric world.

ALEXANDER GRAHAM BELL

(b. March 3, 1847, Edinburgh, Scot.—d. Aug. 2, 1922, Beinn Bhreagh, Cape Breton Island, Nova Scotia, Can.)

Alexander Graham Bell was a Scottish-born American audiologist best known as the inventor of the telephone (1876). For two generations his family had been recognized as leading authorities in elocution and speech correction, with Alexander Melville Bell's *Standard Elocutionist* passing through nearly 200 editions in English. Young Bell and his two brothers were trained to continue the family profession. His early achievements on behalf of the deaf and his invention of the telephone before his 30th birthday bear testimony to the thoroughness of his training.

Alexander ("Graham" was not added until he was 11) was the second of the three sons of Alexander Melville Bell and Eliza Grace Symonds Bell. Apart from one year at a private school, two years at Edinburgh's Royal High School (from which he was graduated at 14), and attendance at a few lectures at Edinburgh University and at University College in London, Bell was largely family trained and self-taught. His first professional post was at Mr. Skinner's school in Elgin, County Moray, where he instructed the children in both music and elocution. In 1864 he became a resident master in Elgin's Weston House

Alexander Graham Bell, who patented the telephone in 1876, inaugurating the 944-mile (1,520 km) telephone link between New York City and Chicago on October 18, 1892.

Academy, where he conducted his first studies in sound. Appropriately, Bell had begun professionally as he would continue through life—as a teacher-scientist.

In 1868 he became his father's assistant in London and assumed full charge while the senior Bell lectured in America. The shock of the sudden death of his older brother from tuberculosis, which had also struck down his younger brother, and the strain of his professional duties soon took their toll on young Bell. Concern for their only surviving son prompted the family's move to Canada in August 1870, where, after settling near Brantford, Ontario, Bell's health rapidly improved.

In 1871 Bell spent several weeks in Boston, lecturing and demonstrating the system of his father's *Visible Speech*, published in 1866, as a means of teaching speech to the deaf. Each phonetic symbol indicated a definite position of the organs of speech such as lips, tongue, and soft palate and could be used by the deaf to imitate the sounds of speech in the usual way. Young A. Graham Bell, as he now preferred to be known, showed, using his father's system, that speech could be taught to the deaf. His astounding results soon led to further invitations to lecture.

Even while vacationing at his parents' home Bell continued his experiments with sound. In 1872 he opened his own school in Boston for training teachers of the deaf, edited his pamphlet *Visible Speech Pioneer*, and continued to study and tutor; in 1873 he became professor of vocal physiology at Boston University.

Never adept with his hands, Bell had the good fortune to discover and inspire Thomas Watson, a young repair mechanic and model maker, who assisted him enthusiastically in devising an apparatus for transmitting sound by electricity. Their long nightly sessions began to produce tangible results. The fathers of George Sanders and Mabel Hubbard, two deaf students whom he helped, were sufficiently impressed with the young teacher to assist him financially in his scientific pursuits. Nevertheless, during normal working hours Bell and Watson were still obliged to fulfill a busy schedule of professional demands. It is scarcely surprising that Bell's health again suffered. On April 6, 1875, he was granted the patent for his multiple telegraph; but after another exhausting six months of long nightly sessions in the workshop, while maintaining his daily professional schedule, Bell had to return to his parents' home in Canada to recuperate. In September 1875 he began to write the specifications for the telephone. On March 7, 1876, the United States Patent Office granted to Bell Patent Number 174,465 covering "The method of, and apparatus for, transmitting vocal or other sounds telegraphically . . . by causing electrical undulations, similar in form to the vibrations of the air accompanying the said vocal or other sounds."

Within a year followed the commercial application and, a few months later, the first of hundreds of legal suits. Ironically, the telephone—until then all too often regarded as a joke and its creator-prophet as, at best, an eccentric—was the subject of the most involved patent litigation in history. The most noteworthy contemporaries of Bell were Antonio Meucci, who filed a caveat (rather than a full patent) in 1871 and let it lapse through lack of funds, and Elisha Gray, who filed a caveat on February 14, 1876, just a few hours after Bell submitted a patent claim. In recognition of Meucci's earlier work, the U.S. House of Representatives passed a resolution on June 11, 2002, honoring his work. The two most celebrated of the early actions were the Dowd and Drawbaugh cases wherein the fledgling Bell Telephone Company successfully challenged two subsidiaries of the giant Western Union Telegraph Company for patent infringement. The charges and accusations were especially painful to Bell's Scottish integrity, but the outcome of all the litigation, which persisted throughout the life of his patents, was that Bell's claims were upheld as the first to conceive and apply the undulatory current. In 1877 Bell married Mabel Hubbard, 10 years his junior.

Beyond the Telephone

The Bell story does not end with the invention of the telephone; indeed, in many ways it was a beginning. A resident of Washington, D.C., Bell continued his experiments in communication, which culminated in the invention of the photophone—transmission of sound on a beam of light; in medical research; and in techniques for teaching speech to the deaf.

In 1880 France honored Bell with the Volta Prize; and the 50,000 francs (roughly equivalent to U.S. $10,000) financed the Volta Laboratory, where, in association with Charles Sumner Tainter and his cousin, Chichester A. Bell, Bell invented the graphophone. Employing an engraving stylus, controllable speeds, and wax cylinders and disks, the graphophone presented a practical approach to sound recording. Bell's share of the royalties financed the Volta Bureau and the American Association to Promote the Teaching of Speech to the Deaf (since 1956 the Alexander Graham Bell Association for the Deaf). May 8, 1893, was one of Bell's happiest days; his 13-year-old prodigy, Helen Keller, participated in the groundbreaking ceremonies for the new Volta Bureau building—today an international information center relating to the oral education of the deaf.

In 1885 Bell acquired land on Cape Breton Island in Nova Scotia. There, in surroundings reminiscent of his early years in Scotland, he established a summer home, Beinn Bhreagh, complete with research laboratories.

In 1898 Bell succeeded his father-in-law as president of the National Geographic Society. Convinced that geography could be taught through pictures, he sought to promote an understanding of life in distant lands in an age when travel was limited to a privileged few. Again he found the proper hands, Gilbert Grosvenor, his future son-in-law, who transformed a modest pamphlet into a unique educational journal reaching millions throughout the world.

As interest in the possibility of flight increased after the turn of the century, he experimented with giant man-carrying kites. Characteristically, Bell again found a group of four willing young enthusiasts to execute his theories. Always an inspiration, Mabel Hubbard Bell, wishing to maintain the stimulating influence of the group, soon founded the Aerial Experiment Association, the first research organization established and endowed by a woman. Deafness was no handicap to the wife of Professor Bell. At Beinn Bhreagh, Bell entered new subjects of investigation, such as sonar detection, solar distillation, the tetrahedron as a structural unit, and hydrofoil craft, one of which weighed more than 10,000 pounds and attained a speed record of 70 miles per hour in 1919.

Apart from his lifelong association with the cause of the deaf, Bell never lingered on one project. His research interests centered on basic principles rather than on refinements. The most cursory examination of his many notebooks shows marginal memos and jottings, often totally unrelated to the subject at hand—reminders of questions and ideas he wanted to investigate. It was impossible for him to carry each of his creative ideas through to a practical end. Many of his conceptions are only today seeing fruition; indeed, some undoubtedly have yet to be developed. The range of his inventive genius is represented only in part by the 18 patents granted in his name alone and the 12 he shared with his collaborators. These included 14 for the telephone and telegraph, 4 for the photophone, 1 for the phonograph, 5 for aerial vehicles, 4 for hydroairplanes, and 2 for a selenium cell.

Until a few days before his death Bell continued to make entries in his journal. During his last dictation he was reassured with "Don't hurry," to which he replied, "I have to."

OTTO LILIENTHAL

(b. May 23, 1848, Anklam, Prussia [now in Ger.]—d. Aug. 10, 1896, Berlin)

Otto Lilienthal was a German aviation pioneer, the most significant aeronautical pioneer in the years leading up to the debut of the American Wright brothers.

Trained as a mechanical engineer, Lilienthal established his own machine shop and flight factory following service in the Franco-German War. Lilienthal began to conduct studies of the forces operating on wings in a stream of air in the late 1870s. The results of that research appeared in 1889 in a book entitled *Der Vogelflug als Grundlage der Fliegekunst* ("Bird Flight as the Basis of Aviation") and in an important series of articles that provided a foundation for the final effort to achieve mechanical flight. As transmitted by Octave Chanute, Lilienthal's friend and American correspondent, the tables of data served as the starting point for the earliest aircraft designs of the Wright brothers.

Having explored the physical principles governing winged flight, Lilienthal began to design and build gliders

Although it may be apocryphal, stories say that Lilienthal's last words were "Sacrifices must be made."

on the basis of the information he had gathered. Between 1891 and 1896, he completed some 2,000 flights in at least 16 distinct glider types. The largest number of flights were made with his standard glider, a monoplane aircraft with a stabilizing tail at the rear and wings that resembled "the outspread pinions of a soaring bird." The wing ribs and other covered portions of the aircraft were usually constructed of split willow. The wing covering was cotton twill shirting, doped with a colloidal solution to make it more airtight. In the standard glider, the operator hung suspended between the two halves of the wing. The operator shifted his weight to move the center of gravity and exercise some measure of control over the motion of the craft. Although Lilienthal recognized the danger and inadequacy of this method of flight control and gave some thought to alternative systems, he did not develop or test them. Lilienthal sold several standard gliders to other experimenters as far distant as Russia and the United States.

Lilienthal's career as a builder and pilot of gliders coincided with the development of high-speed and stroboscopic photography. Images of Lilienthal flying through the air aboard his standard glider appeared around the globe in newspapers and the great illustrated magazines of the period. Those pictures convinced millions of readers in Europe and the United States that the age of flight was at hand. Lilienthal broke his back in a glider crash on August 9, 1896, and died in a Berlin hospital the next day.

EMIL BERLINER

(b. May 20, 1851, Hannover [now in Ger.]—d. Aug. 3, 1929, Washington, D.C., U.S.)

Emil (or Emile) Berliner, a German-born American inventor, made important contributions to microphone technology and developed the gramophone, the first viable disc-type record player.

Berliner immigrated to the United States in 1870. In 1877, a year after Alexander Graham Bell invented the telephone, Berliner, while working as a clerk in Washington, D.C., developed a transmitter employing a loose metal contact separated by a layer of carbon. The device did not perform well as a telephone transmitter, as Berliner was later to admit. Nevertheless, the rights to the invention were purchased by the Bell Telephone Company, which used it to develop the carbon microphone—thus earning Berliner a dubious reputation as the "inventor of the microphone."

In 1884, after several years' association with Bell Telephone, Berliner established his own independent laboratory in Washington. There he made another contribution of major significance: the flat recording disc, on which a spiral recording groove was inscribed by a stylus that moved laterally, rather than vertically, thus producing excellent sound on a surface that could be manufactured more efficiently than Edison-type cylinder recordings. Berliner patented his invention, which he called the Gramophone, in 1887. He then embarked on a series of efforts to establish gramophone businesses in North America and Europe, all the while working on methods to improve the recording and disc-replicating process. The machine itself would not be perfected until after 1896, the year that Eldridge Johnson began to make spring-driven players for the Berliner Gramophone Company. The Berliner Gramophone Company supplied machines and recorded discs to the independent National Gramophone Company, which in turn sold the products in the United States. In 1897 the Gramophone Company, Ltd., was started up in London and the Gram-o-Phone Company was established in Montreal. In 1898 Berliner, with his brothers Joseph and Jacob, founded the Deutsche Grammophon Gesellshaft manufacturing plant in Hannover.

In 1901 Berliner pooled his patent and trademark rights with those of Eldridge Johnson, who formed the Victor Talking Machine Company. Berliner subsequently became interested in aeronautics; in 1908 he designed a lightweight internal-combustion engine that became a widely imitated prototype power plant for aircraft. Under his general supervision, his son, Henry Berliner, designed a helicopter that flew successfully as early as 1919. Returning to problems of sound reproduction, the elder Berliner in 1925 invented an acoustic tile for use in auditoriums and concert halls.

NIKOLA TESLA

(b. July 9/10, 1856, Smiljan, Austria-Hungary [now in Croatia]—d. Jan. 7, 1943, New York City, N.Y., U.S.)

Nikola Tesla was a Serbian-American inventor and engineer who discovered and patented the rotating magnetic field, the basis of most alternating-current machinery. He also developed the three-phase system of electric power transmission. He immigrated to the United States in 1884 and sold the patent rights to his system of alternating-current dynamos, transformers, and motors to George Westinghouse. In 1891 he invented the Tesla coil, an induction coil widely used in radio technology.

Tesla was from a family of Serbian origin. His father was an Orthodox priest; his mother was unschooled but highly intelligent. As he matured, he displayed remarkable imagination and creativity as well as a poetic touch.

Training for an engineering career, he attended the Technical University at Graz, Austria, and the University of Prague. At Graz he first saw the Gramme dynamo, which operated as a generator and, when reversed, became an electric motor, and he conceived a way to use alternating current to advantage. Later, at Budapest, he visualized the principle of the rotating magnetic field and developed plans for an induction motor that would become his first step toward the successful utilization of alternating current. In 1882 Tesla went to work in Paris for the Continental Edison Company, and, while on assignment to Strassburg in 1883, he constructed, in after-work hours, his first induction motor. Tesla sailed for America in 1884 arriving in New York with four cents in his pocket, a few of his own poems, and calculations for a flying machine. He first found employment with Thomas Edison, but the two inventors were far apart in background and methods, and their separation was inevitable.

In May 1885, George Westinghouse, head of the Westinghouse Electric Company in Pittsburgh, bought the patent rights to Tesla's polyphase system of alternating-current dynamos, transformers, and motors. The transaction precipitated a titanic power struggle between Edison's direct-current systems and the Tesla–Westinghouse alternating-current approach, which eventually won out.

Tesla soon established his own laboratory, where his inventive mind could be given free rein. He experimented with shadowgraphs similar to those that later were to be used by Wilhelm Röntgen when he discovered X-rays in 1895. Tesla's countless experiments included work on a carbon button lamp, on the power of electrical resonance, and on various types of lighting.

In order to allay fears of alternating currents, Tesla gave exhibitions in his laboratory in which he lit lamps by allowing electricity to flow through his body. He was often invited to lecture at home and abroad. The Tesla coil, which he invented in 1891, is widely used today in radio

This photograph of Tesla was taken around 1890. Tesla became a naturalized American citizen in 1891.

and television sets and other electronic equipment. That year also marked the date of Tesla's U.S. citizenship.

Westinghouse used Tesla's alternating current system to light the World's Columbian Exposition at Chicago in 1893. This success was a factor in their winning the contract to install the first power machinery at Niagara Falls, which bore Tesla's name and patent numbers. The project carried power to Buffalo, New York, by 1896.

In 1898 Tesla announced his invention of a teleautomatic boat guided by remote control. When skepticism was voiced, Tesla proved his claims for it before a crowd in Madison Square Garden.

In Colorado Springs, Colorado, where he stayed from May 1899 until early 1900, Tesla made what he regarded as his most important discovery—terrestrial stationary waves. By this discovery he proved that the earth could be used as a conductor and made to resonate at a certain electrical frequency. He also lit 200 lamps without wires from a distance of 25 miles (40 km) and created man-made lightning, producing flashes measuring 135 feet (41 m). At one time he was certain he had received signals from another planet in his Colorado laboratory, a claim that was met with derision in some scientific journals.

Returning to New York in 1900, Tesla began construction on Long Island of a wireless world broadcasting tower, with $150,000 capital from the American financier J. Pierpont Morgan. Tesla claimed he secured the loan by assigning 51 percent of his patent rights of telephony and telegraphy to Morgan. He expected to provide worldwide communication and to furnish facilities for sending pictures, messages, weather warnings, and stock reports. The project was abandoned because of a financial panic, labor troubles, and Morgan's withdrawal of support. It was Tesla's greatest defeat.

Tesla's work then shifted to turbines and other projects. Because of a lack of funds, his ideas remained in his notebooks, which are still examined by enthusiasts for unexploited clues. In 1915 he was severely disappointed when a report that he and Edison were to share the Nobel Prize proved erroneous. Tesla was the recipient of the Edison Medal in 1917, the highest honor that the American Institute of Electrical Engineers could bestow.

Tesla allowed himself only a few close friends. Among them were the writers Robert Underwood Johnson, Mark Twain, and Francis Marion Crawford. He was quite impractical in financial matters and an eccentric, driven by compulsions and a progressive germ phobia. But he had a way of intuitively sensing hidden scientific secrets and employing his inventive talent to prove his hypotheses. Tesla was a godsend to reporters who sought sensational copy but a problem to editors who were uncertain how seriously his futuristic prophecies should be regarded. Caustic criticism greeted his speculations concerning communication with other planets, his assertions that he could split the Earth like an apple, and his claim of having invented a death ray capable of destroying 10,000 airplanes at a distance of 250 miles (400 km).

After Tesla's death the custodian of alien property impounded his trunks, which held his papers, his diplomas and other honors, his letters, and his laboratory notes. These were eventually inherited by Tesla's nephew, Sava Kosanovich, and later housed in the Nikola Tesla Museum in Belgrade. Hundreds filed into New York City's Cathedral of Saint John the Divine for his funeral services, acknowledging the loss of a great genius. Three Nobel Prize recipients addressed their tribute to "one of the outstanding intellects of the world who paved the way for many of the technological developments of modern times."

RUDOLF DIESEL

(b. March 18, 1858, Paris, France—d. Sept. 29, 1913, at sea in the English Channel)

Rudolf Christian Karl Diesel was a German thermal engineer who invented the internal-combustion engine that bears his name. He was also a distinguished connoisseur of the arts, a linguist, and a social theorist.

Diesel, the son of German-born parents, grew up in Paris until the family was deported to England in 1870 following the outbreak of the Franco-German War. From London Diesel was sent to Augsburg, his father's native town, to continue his schooling. There and later at the Technische Hochschule (Technical High School) in Munich he established a brilliant scholastic record in fields of engineering. At Munich he was a protégé of the refrigeration engineer Carl von Linde, whose Paris firm he joined in 1880.

Diesel devoted much of his time to the self-imposed task of developing an internal combustion engine that would approach the theoretical efficiency of the Carnot cycle. For a time he experimented with an expansion engine using ammonia. About 1890, in which year he moved to a new post with the Linde firm in Berlin, he conceived the idea for the diesel engine. He obtained a German development patent in 1892 and the following year published a description of his engine under the title *Theorie und Konstruktion eines rationellen Wäremotors* (*Theory and Construction of a Rational Heat Motor*). With support from the Maschinenfabrik Augsburg and the Krupp firms, he produced a series of increasingly successful models, culminating in his demonstration in 1897 of a 25-horsepower, four-stroke, single vertical cylinder compression engine. The high efficiency of Diesel's engine, together with its comparative simplicity of design, made it an immediate commercial success, and royalty fees brought great wealth to its inventor.

Diesel disappeared from the deck of the mail steamer *Dresden* en route to London and was assumed to have drowned.

GEORGE WASHINGTON CARVER

(b. 1861?, near Diamond Grove, Mo., U.S.—d. Jan. 5, 1943, Tuskegee, Ala.)

George Washington Carver was an American agricultural chemist, agronomist, and experimenter whose development of new products derived from peanuts (groundnuts), sweet potatoes, and soybeans helped revolutionize the agricultural economy of the South. For most of his career he taught and conducted research at the Tuskegee Normal and Industrial Institute (now Tuskegee University) in Tuskegee, Alabama.

Carver was the son of an enslaved woman owned by Moses Carver. During the Civil War, slave owners found it difficult to hold enslave people in the border state of Missouri, and Moses Carver therefore sent his, including the young child and his mother, to Arkansas. After the war, Moses Carver learned that all of them had disappeared except for a child named George. Frail and sick, the motherless child was returned to his former master's home and nursed back to health. The boy had a delicate sense of color and form and learned to draw; later in life he devoted considerable time to painting flowers, plants, and landscapes. Though the Carvers told him he was no longer enslaved, he remained on their plantation until he was about 10 or 12 years old, when he left to acquire an education. He spent some time wandering about, working with his hands and developing his keen interest in plants and animals.

By both books and experience, George acquired a

Carver transformed the agricultural practices of the South and gained a reputation as one of the most important scientists of the era.

fragmentary education while doing whatever work came to hand in order to subsist. He supported himself by varied occupations that included general household worker, hotel cook, laundryman, farm laborer, and homesteader. In his late 20s he managed to obtain a high school education in Minneapolis, Kansas, while working as a farmhand. After a university in Kansas refused to admit him because he was Black, Carver matriculated at Simpson College, Indianola, Iowa, where he studied piano and art, subsequently transferring to Iowa State Agricultural College (Ames, Iowa), where he received a bachelor's degree in agricultural science in 1894 and a master of science degree in 1896.

Carver left Iowa for Alabama in the fall of 1896 to direct the newly organized department of agriculture at the Tuskegee Normal and Industrial Institute, a school headed by the noted Black American educator Booker T. Washington. At Tuskegee, Washington was trying to improve the lot of Black Americans through education and the acquisition of useful skills rather than through political agitation; he stressed conciliation, compromise, and economic development as the paths for Black advancement in American society. Despite many offers elsewhere, Carver would remain at Tuskegee for the rest of his life.

After becoming the institute's director of agricultural research in 1896, Carver devoted his time to research projects aimed at helping Southern agriculture, demonstrating ways in which farmers could improve their economic situation. He conducted experiments in soil management and crop production and directed an experimental farm. At this time agriculture in the Deep South was in serious trouble because the unremitting single-crop cultivation of cotton had left the soil of many fields exhausted and worthless, and erosion had then taken its toll on areas that could no longer sustain any plant cover. As a remedy, Carver urged Southern farmers to plant peanuts and soybeans, which, since they belong to the legume family, could restore nitrogen to the soil while also providing the protein so badly needed in the diet of many Southerners. Carver found that Alabama's soils were particularly well-suited to growing peanuts and sweet potatoes, but when the state's farmers began cultivating these crops instead of cotton, they found little demand for them on the market. In response to this problem, Carver set about enlarging the commercial possibilities of the peanut and sweet potato through a long and ingenious program of laboratory research. He ultimately developed 300 derivative products from peanuts—among them cheese, milk, coffee, flour, ink, dyes, plastics, wood stains, soap, linoleum, medicinal oils, and cosmetics—and 118 from sweet potatoes, including flour, vinegar, molasses, rubber, ink, a synthetic rubber, and postage stamp glue.

In 1914, at a time when the boll weevil had almost ruined cotton growers, Carver revealed his experiments to the public, and increasing numbers of the South's farmers began to turn to peanuts, sweet potatoes, and their derivatives for income. Much exhausted land was renewed, and the South became a major new supplier of agricultural products. When Carver arrived at Tuskegee in 1896, the peanut had not even been recognized as a crop, but within the next half century it became one of the six leading crops throughout the United States and, in the South, the second cash crop (after cotton) by 1940. In 1942 the U.S. government allotted 5,000,000 acres of peanuts to farmers. Carver's efforts had finally helped liberate the South from its excessive dependence on cotton.

Among Carver's many honors were his election to Britain's Society for the Encouragement of Arts,

Manufactures, and Commerce (London) in 1916 and his receipt of the Spingarn Medal in 1923. Late in his career he declined an invitation to work for Thomas A. Edison at a salary of more than $100,000 a year. Presidents Calvin Coolidge and Franklin D. Roosevelt visited him, and his friends included Henry Ford and Mohandas K. Gandhi. Foreign governments requested his counsel on agricultural matters: Joseph Stalin, for example, in 1931 invited him to superintend cotton plantations in southern Russia and to make a tour of the Soviet Union, but Carver refused.

In 1940 Carver donated his life savings to the establishment of the Carver Research Foundation at Tuskegee for continuing research in agriculture. During World War II he worked to replace the textile dyes formerly imported from Europe, and in all he produced dyes of 500 different shades.

Many scientists thought of Carver more as a concoctionist than as a contributor to scientific knowledge. Many of his fellow Blacks were critical of what they regarded as his subservience. Certainly, this small, mild, soft-spoken, innately modest man, eccentric in dress and mannerism, seemed unbelievably heedless of the conventional pleasures and rewards of this life. But these qualities endeared Carver to many whites, who were almost invariably charmed by his humble demeanor and his quiet work in self-imposed segregation at Tuskegee. As a result of his accommodation to the mores of the South, whites came to regard him with a sort of patronizing adulation.

Carver thus increasingly came to stand for much of white America as a kind of saintly and comfortable symbol of the intellectual achievements of Black Americans. Carver was evidently uninterested in the role his image played in the racial politics of the time. His great desire in later life was simply to serve humanity; and his work, which began for the sake of the poorest of the Black sharecroppers, paved the way for a better life for the entire South. His efforts brought about a significant advance in agricultural training in an era when agriculture was the largest single occupation of Americans, and he extended Tuskegee's influence throughout the South by encouraging improved farm methods, crop diversification, and soil conservation.

JAMES A. NAISMITH

(b. Nov. 6, 1861, Almonte, Ont., Can.—d. Nov. 28, 1939, Lawrence, Kan., U.S.)

James A. Naismith was a Canadian-American physical-education director who, in December 1891, at the International Young Men's Christian Association Training School, afterward Springfield (Massachusetts) College, invented the game of basketball.

As a young man, Naismith (who had no middle name but adopted the initial "A.") studied theology and excelled in various sports. In the autumn of 1891 he was appointed an instructor by Luther Halsey Gulick Jr. head of the Physical Education Department at Springfield. Gulick asked Naismith and other instructors to devise indoor games that could replace the boring or dangerous exercises used at the school during the winter. For his new game Naismith selected features of soccer, American football, field hockey, and other outdoor sports but (in theory) eliminated body contact between players. Because his physical education class at that time was composed of 18 men, basketball originally was played by nine on each side (eventually reduced to five).

For that first game of basketball in 1891, Naismith used as goals two half-bushel peach baskets, which gave the sport its name. The students were enthusiastic. After

Naismith, shown here, chose a soccer ball for the first basketball game.

much running and shooting, William R. Chase made a midcourt shot—the only score in that historic contest. Word spread about the newly invented game, and numerous associations wrote Naismith for a copy of the rules, which were published in the January 15, 1892, issue of the *Triangle*, the YMCA Training School's campus paper. Naismith's original rules, prohibiting walking or running with the ball and limiting physical contact, are still the basis of a game that spread throughout the world.

In 1898 Naismith received an M.D. from Gross Medical College, Denver, Colorado, afterward the University of Colorado School of Medicine. From that year until 1937 he was chairman of the physical education department at the University of Kansas, Lawrence, where he also coached basketball until 1908. In addition to basketball, he is credited with inventing the protective helmet for football players. The Naismith Memorial Basketball Hall of Fame, in Springfield, Massachusetts, was incorporated in 1959.

AUGUSTE AND LOUIS LUMIÈRE

respectively, (b. Oct. 19, 1862, Besançon, France—d. April 10, 1954, Lyon); (b. Oct. 5, 1864, Besançon, France—d. June 6, 1948, Bandol)

The Lumière brothers, Auguste and Louis, were French inventors and pioneer manufacturers of photographic equipment who devised an early motion-picture camera and projector called the Cinématographe (*cinema* is derived from this name). The two brothers created the film *La Sortie des ouvriers de l'usine Lumière* (1895; "Workers Leaving the Lumière Factory"), which is considered the first motion picture.

Sons of a painter turned photographer, the Lumière brothers displayed brilliance in science at school in Lyon, where their father had settled. Louis worked on the problem of commercially satisfactory development of film; at 18 he had succeeded so well that with his father's financial aid he opened a factory for producing photographic plates, which gained immediate success. By 1894 the Lumières were producing some 15,000,000 plates a year. That year the father, Antoine, was invited to a showing of Thomas Edison's Kinetoscope in Paris; his description of the peephole machine on his return to Lyon set Louis and Auguste to work on the problem of combining animation with projection. Louis found the solution, which was patented in 1895. At that time they attached less importance to this invention than to improvements they had made simultaneously in color photography. But on December 28, 1895, a showing at the Grand Café on the boulevard des Capucines in Paris brought wide public acclaim and the beginning of the history of cinema.

The Lumière apparatus consisted of a single camera used for both photographing and projecting at 16 frames per second. Their first films (they made more than 40 during 1896) recorded everyday French life—e.g., the arrival of a train, a game of cards, a toiling blacksmith, the feeding of a baby, soldiers marching, the activity of a city street. Others were early comedy shorts. The Lumières presented the first newsreel, a film of the French Photographic Society Conference, and the first documentaries, four films about the Lyon fire department. Beginning in 1896 they sent a trained crew of innovative cameraman-projectionists to cities throughout the world to show films and shoot new material.

REGINALD FESSENDEN

(b. Oct. 6, 1866, Milton, Que., Can.—d. July 22, 1932, Hamilton, Bermuda)

Reginald Aubrey Fessenden was a Canadian-American radio pioneer who broadcast the first program of music and voice ever transmitted over long distances.

After study at Trinity College School, in Port Hope, Ontario, and Bishop's College in Lennoxville, Quebec, Fessenden went to Bermuda as principal of the Whitney Institute, where he developed an interest in science that led him to resign and go to New York. Working as a tester at the Thomas Edison Machine Works, he met Thomas Edison and in 1887 became chief chemist of the Edison Laboratory at Orange, New Jersey. In 1890 he became chief electrician at the Westinghouse works at Pittsfield, Massachusetts, and in 1892 turned to an academic career, as professor of electrical engineering first at Purdue University, West Lafayette, Indiana, then at the Western University of Pennsylvania (now the University of Pittsburgh), where he worked on the problem of wireless communication.

In 1900 Fessenden left the university to conduct experiments in wireless telegraphy for the U.S. Weather Bureau, which wanted to adapt radiotelegraphy to weather forecasting. He then became interested in voice transmission and developed the idea of superimposing electric waves, vibrating at the frequencies of sound waves, upon a constant radio frequency, so as to modulate the amplitude of the radio wave into the shape of the sound wave. (This is the principle of amplitude modulation, or AM.) Fessenden also invented an electrolytic radio detector sensitive enough for use in radiotelephony.

In 1902 Fessenden joined two financiers in organizing the National Electric Signalling Company to manufacture his inventions. He directed Ernst Alexanderson of the General Electric Company in building a 50,000-hertz alternator that made possible the realization of radiotelephony, and Fessenden at once built a transmitting station at Brant Rock, Massachusetts. On December 24, 1906, wireless operators as far away as Norfolk, Virginia, were startled to hear speech and music from Brant Rock through their own receivers. That same year, Fessenden established two-way transatlantic wireless telegraphic communication between Brant Rock and Scotland.

Fessenden further contributed in 1902 to the development of radio by demonstrating the heterodyne principle of converting high-frequency wireless signals to a lower frequency that is more easily controlled and amplified. This was the forerunner of the superheterodyne principle, which made easy tuning of radio signals possible and was a critical factor for the growth of commercial broadcasting.

Fessenden has also been credited with inventing the radio compass, the sonic depth finder, submarine signalling devices, and the turboelectric drive for battleships.

Glossary

antithesis: The exact opposite.

ballast: Used to give balance or change the center of gravity in ships or planes.

deprecate: To criticize.

derivative: Describing something that is or has elements that were first used for something else.

dirigible: An airship.

elocution: The study of how to speak clearly.

inchoate: Not fully formed.

induction: The process through which an electric current is produced in objects.

infringe: To fail to obey or act in agreement with a rule or law.

ingenuity: Creativity, skill, and cleverness in solving problems.

litigation: The act, process, or practice of settling a dispute in a court of law.

patent: Rights given to a person by the government to make, use, or sell an invention.

quintessential: Perfectly typical or representative of a particular kind of person or thing.

reify: To give form to an idea.

serendipity: Luck in unexpectedly finding valuable things.

supersede: To take the place of something else.

For More Information

BOOKS

Hearst, Michael. *Unconventional Vehicles*. San Francisco, CA: Chronicle Books, 2021.

Keppeler, Jill. *Helen Keller and Alexander Graham Bell.* New York, NY: Gareth Stevens Publishing, 2022.

Naismith, James. *The James Naismith Reader: Basketball in His Own Words.* Lincoln, NE: University of Nebraska Press, 2021.

Parkin, Michelle. *George Washington Carver.* Chicago, IL: Norwood House Press, 2023.

WEBSITES

Library of Congress: Life of Thomas Alva Edison
www.loc.gov/collections/edison-company-motion-pictures-and-sound-recordings/articles-and-essays/biography/life-of-thomas-alva-edison/
Read a biography of Thomas Edison and learn more about his revolutionary inventions.

National Geographic: How the Lumière Brothers Invented the Movies
www.nationalgeographic.com/history/history-magazine/article/creation-of-the-motion-picture-lumiere-brothers
Read more about how the Lumière brothers were trailblazers in the art and science of photography and motion pictures.

Nikola Tesla Museum
tesla-museum.org/en/home/
Find out more about Nikola Tesla and his extraordinary ideas and achievements.

Zeppelin Museum
www.zeppelin-museum.de/en
Investigate the inventions on display at the Zeppelin Museum.

Index

agriculture, 49–54
aircraft, 6–9, 12, 39, 41, 43, 47
alternating current, 43–46
American Civil War, 21, 49
American inventors, 10–12, 19–39, 41–47, 49–56, 57–59
automobiles, 14–18, 30

basketball, 54–56
batteries, 20, 28, 30, 32

Canadian inventors, 54–59

deafness, 20–21, 32–33, 35, 37–38
dirigibles, 6–9

electricity, 13, 18, 20, 25, 27, 30–31, 35, 43–44
electric lights, 20, 24–28, 31

flight, 6–9, 12, 38–41, 43, 47
Franco-German War, 7, 39, 48
French inventors, 56–57

gasoline engines, 7, 14
German inventors, 6–9, 14–19, 39–43, 48–49
gramophones, 42–43
graphophones, 28, 37

internal-combustion engines, 12, 14, 16, 43, 48–49
Irish inventors, 12–13

Kinetoscope, 30, 57

machine guns, 10–12
microphones, 42
motion pictures, 28, 30, 56–57

Nobel Prizes, 18, 47

Paris Exposition, 10
patents, 10, 12, 15, 20, 23, 27, 31–32, 34, 36–37, 39, 42–44, 46, 48, 57
phonographs, 20, 22–24, 28–30
photography, 19, 30, 41, 56–57

radio, 43–44, 57–59
railroads, 20–22
rotating magnetic field, 43–44

Scottish inventors, 33–39
Serbian inventors, 43–47
silent movies, 30
slavery, 49
sports, 54–56
steam engines, 7, 12–13
submarines, 13, 30, 59

telegraphs, 20–21, 58
telephones, 23–24, 33–37, 42
Tesla coil, 43–44
transcontinental flight, 9

U.S. Navy, 13

weapons, 10–13
World War I, 12
World War II, 53

X-rays, 18–19